ANIMALS ON THE BRINK

Leatherback Turtles

E. Melanie Watt

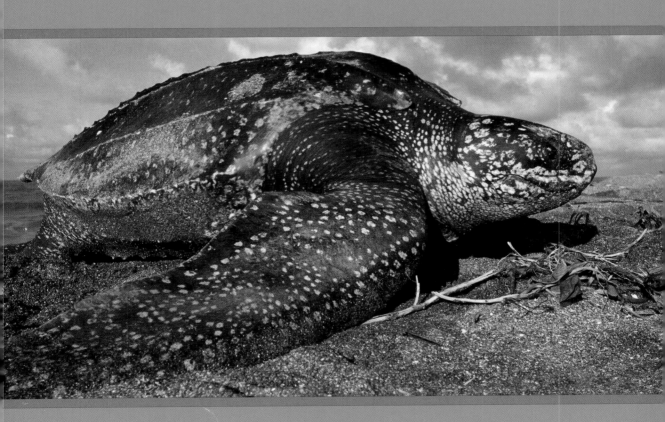

MEDIA ENHANCED BOOKS

AV2 BY WEIGL

ADDED VALUE • AUDIO VISUAL

www.av2books.com

AV² provides enriched content that supplements and complements this book. Weigl's AV² books strive to create inspired learning and engage young minds in a total learning experience.

Your AV² Media Enhanced books come alive with...

Go to **www.av2books.com**, and enter this book's unique code.

BOOK CODE

R 6 3 6 6 4 8

AV² by Weigl brings you media enhanced books that support active learning.

Audio
Listen to sections of the book read aloud.

Video
Watch informative video clips.

Embedded Weblinks
Gain additional information for research.

Try This!
Complete activities and hands-on experiments.

Key Words
Study vocabulary, and complete a matching word activity.

Quizzes
Test your knowledge.

Slide Show
View images and captions, and prepare a presentation.

... and much, much more!

Published by AV² by Weigl
350 5th Avenue, 59th Floor
New York, NY 10118
Website: www.av2books.com   www.weigl.com

Library of Congress Cataloguing in Publication data available upon request.
Fax 1-866-449-3445 for the attention of the Publishing Records department.

ISBN 978-1-61913-427-0 (hard cover)
ISBN 978-1-61913-428-7 (soft cover)

Printed in the United States of America in North Mankato, Minnesota
1 2 3 4 5 6 7 8 9 16 15 14 13 12

052012
WEP170512

Project Coordinator Aaron Carr
Design Mandy Christiansen

Every reasonable effort has been made to trace ownership and to obtain permission to reprint copyright material. The publishers would be pleased to have any errors or omissions brought to their attention so that they may be corrected in subsequent printings.

Photo Credits
Weigl acknowledges Getty Images as its primary photo supplier for this title.

Contents

Take a Stand
Debate • Research

How to take a stand on an issue   **5**

Should people be restricted
  from using the turtles' nesting
  beaches?   **17**

Should the tagging of turtles
  be stopped because the
  information tagging provides
  is not very useful?   **29**

Should people be allowed to
  eat some leatherback
  turtle eggs?   **33**

The Leatherback Turtle

The leatherback turtle is the largest turtle in the world. Adult leatherbacks can weigh more than 2,000 pounds (900 kilograms) and be more than 7 feet (2.1 meters) long. This makes the leatherback one of the largest living reptiles. In addition, the leatherback turtle is found in more places throughout the world than any other reptile.

In this book you will see how a leatherback **hatchling** grows into a giant reptile. You will learn where leatherbacks live, what they eat, and what problems each hatchling must overcome to reach adulthood. You will discover how the leatherback was named. You will also find out why the leatherback's future is in question, and what you can do to help this **endangered** animal.

The number of leatherback turtles has been declining. The leatherback turtle is considered endangered by the U.S. government and critically endangered by the International Union for Conservation of Nature.

By some measures, the leatherback is the largest reptile. Though not as long as the Australian saltwater crocodile or the Komodo dragon, the leatherback tends to weigh the most of the three largest reptiles.

How to Take a Stand on an Issue

Research is important to the study of any scientific field. When scientists choose a subject to study, they must conduct research to ensure they have a thorough understanding of the topic. They ask questions about the subject and then search for answers. Sometimes, however, there is no clear answer to a question. In these cases, scientists must use the information they have to form a hypothesis, or theory. They must take a stand on one side of an issue or the other. Follow the process below for each Take a Stand section in this book to determine where you stand on these issues.

1. **What Is the Issue?**
   a. Determine a research subject, and form a general question about the subject.

2. **Form a Hypothesis**
   a. Search at the library and online for sources of information on the subject.
   b. Conduct basic research on the subject to narrow down the general question.
   c. Form a hypothesis on the subject based on research to this point.
   d. Make predictions based on the hypothesis. What are the expected results?

3. **Research the Issue**
   a. Conduct extensive research using a variety of sources, including books, scientific journals, and reliable websites.
   b. Collect data on the issue and take notes on all information gathered from research.
   c. Draw conclusions based on the information collected.

4. **Conclusion**
   a. Explain the research findings.
   b. Was the hypothesis proved or disproved?

Turtle Truths

Leatherbacks can be as large as a double bed. The largest leatherback ever found was 2,020 pounds (916 kg).

The leatherback's eyelids do not close from bottom to top, as a human's eyelids do. The leatherback turtle's eyelids close from side to side.

Features

Leatherbacks are sea turtles. Although they spend most of their lives in water, sea turtles use lungs to breathe. The leatherback can stay underwater for more than half an hour when resting, but to do so, it must hold its breath. The turtle regularly rises to the surface in order to take in air. Like other sea turtles, leatherbacks lay eggs rather than give birth to live young. Leatherbacks spend most of their time at sea, but they swim to a beach to lay their eggs. When the young hatch, they look like smaller versions of the adults. Breathing air, laying eggs, and having young that look like small adults are normal features for all sea turtles and for most kinds of reptiles. In some other important ways, however, leatherbacks are unique. Leatherback turtles look different from other sea turtles and can dive much deeper. The shells of other sea turtles are made of many hard sections called **scutes**. A leatherback does not have scutes. Instead, it has a shell that is like rubber. Its whole body and shell are covered with a leathery skin. That is why it is called the leatherback, or leathery, turtle. Reptiles change their body temperature to match their surroundings, but leatherbacks can stay somewhat warm even while deep in cold water.

Sea turtles have been around for a long time. They are known to have been alive at least 200 million years ago. They were quite common 130 million years ago and lived at the same time as the dinosaurs. The fossils of one **species** of sea turtle, known as the *Archelon*, have been found in what are now Kansas and South Dakota. The *Archelon* had a shell that was 12 feet (3.7 m) long. It was as big as a small car. The leatherback has been on Earth for about 120 million years. It appears that there were once several different species of leatherback turtles. The species now called the leatherback turtle is the only one of these that is still living today.

Leatherback sea turtles do not survive well in captivity. They do not have the ability to swim backward, so when placed in a tank, they ram into the tank's sides. In nature, most leatherbacks die as hatchlings. Among those that survive the early dangers, at least some leatherbacks have lived 30 or more years. Some leatherbacks have been found on beaches 18 or 19 years after they were first studied by researchers. The turtles were adults when they were first located, so they were much older than 18 or 19 when they were found again. Many researchers believe that leatherbacks can live 40 or more years.

Classification

Today there are more than 250 species of turtles in the world, but only seven or eight species are sea turtles. There are differences between these sea turtle species, but they also share many important features. All sea turtles have special characteristics that help them survive in the sea. They all have streamlined bodies and large flippers. These features help them to dive and to swim. Unlike many other turtle species, sea turtles cannot pull their heads into their shells. This is because sea turtles have less space inside their shells. Their shells are flatter than those of other turtles, to help make sea turtles streamlined for water travel. They also have larger swimming muscles.

Except for leatherbacks, all of the sea turtle species alive today have been grouped by scientists into one **family**. Leatherback turtles are thought to belong to a separate family because of their differences from the other sea turtle species. Not only are their shells different, but their skin is also unique. The skin of other sea turtles has scales, like the skin of other reptiles. These scales are made from the same material as human fingernails and hair. The skin of an adult leatherback does not have scales. The Latin name for leatherback turtles is *Dermochelys coriacea*. *Dermo* means "skin," *chelys* means "turtle," and *coriacea* means "skin-covered."

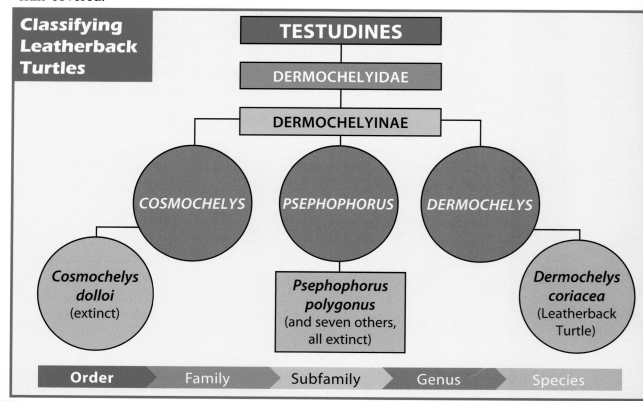

Classifying Leatherback Turtles

TESTUDINES
DERMOCHELYIDAE
DERMOCHELYINAE

COSMOCHELYS — Cosmochelys dolloi (extinct)

PSEPHOPHORUS — Psephophorus polygonus (and seven others, all extinct)

DERMOCHELYS — Dermochelys coriacea (Leatherback Turtle)

Order — Family — Subfamily — Genus — Species

A leatherback's shell differs from other sea turtle shells in size. It also has distinctive ridges running along its length.

The Kemp's ridley turtle has a flattened, round shell compared with the large ridged shell of the leatherback turtle.

Compared with baby loggerhead and green turtles, a baby leatherback is much larger.

Special Adaptations

Leatherback sea turtles have special adaptations that allow them to dive deep into the ocean and to survive in colder water than other sea turtles. The leatherback's adaptations help make it an excellent swimmer and the most widely distributed of all sea turtles.

Shell

Leatherbacks have been reported to dive deeper than 3,330 feet (1,015 m), where the water pressure is very strong. Their stiff but flexible shells allow them to do so. Leatherbacks do not have a hard breastbone or hard lower shell, so they can collapse somewhat in deep water. Their shells are wide across the shoulder area and narrower toward the tail.

Front Flippers

The powerful front flippers pull the turtle forward. The front flippers of an adult are about half the length of its body. The muscles that help move the front flippers can weigh up to one-third of the turtle's total weight.

Blood and Lungs

Adaptations in their blood and lungs also help leatherbacks cope with deep dives. These turtles have a special system that circulates blood in their flippers. This helps them to keep body heat even in very cold water.

Back Flippers

The leatherback's back flippers help it to steer. Its long flipper bones are not as stiff as similar bones in other turtles. For this reason, the bones are less likely to break under strong water pressure. Studies of the leatherback show that it never stops swimming. It probably swims even when asleep.

Skin

The leatherback turtle is so large, it takes a much longer time to become cold in chilly water than a smaller turtle would. In addition, a thick layer of fat under its skin acts as insulation. The smooth, leathery skin on its body and shell helps it move smoothly through water. A large amount of body oil helps to keep the leatherback's body from breaking apart in deep water.

Groups

A large group of turtles drifting or swimming together in the open ocean is called a **flotilla**. Leatherback turtles rarely form flotillas. A total of 174 leatherbacks were seen along 376 miles (605 km) of water off the coast of South Carolina in a recent year, but that was over many days. In another case, about 100 leatherbacks were seen in a 30-mile (48-km) line in coastal waters. In this rare case, the turtles might have come together to feed because there was a school of jellyfish, their favorite food, in the same area. The social behavior of leatherbacks is often described as solitary. Although they may act in a similar manner while near other turtles, these behaviors seem to be driven by individual needs rather than those of the group.

Every few years, the female leatherbacks return to beaches in tropical areas in order to lay eggs. Some species of sea turtles nest in large groups called *arribadas*. This is a Spanish word meaning "arrivals." *Arribadas* of Kemp's ridley turtles were once reported to have hundreds of thousands of females nesting at the same time. Although many female leatherbacks may have the same nesting season, they do not form *arribadas*. They each nest at different times during the nesting season. There may be more than one female with eggs on the same beach, but the mother turtles seem to keep to their own schedules. Leatherbacks seem to operate in their own little worlds most of the time, although this general impression may change as scientists continue to study these turtles.

Beyond courtship and mating, it is believed that individual leatherback turtles rarely interact with one another. At this time, very little is known about their mating rituals either. Scientists are not sure how mates find or choose each other. They also do not know if the mates stay together for a while or if they leave each other right away. The father never has to leave the water, which makes it even harder to study mating behavior. The females are the only ones who come to shore to nest. Despite their large size, leatherback turtles are hard to research in the open sea, in part because they dive so deep and also because they are moving around so much of the time.

Of all the sea turtles, leatherbacks travel over the widest range.

Turtle Truths

A large nesting population of leatherback turtles was recently discovered in Gabon, Africa. In three seasons, more than 41,000 females used the beaches of Gabon.

At birth, a hatchling is surrounded by other hatchlings from the nest. When the males drag themselves into the sea, they will never return to land again.

Communication

Scientists are trying to learn more about communication among leatherbacks. When nesting, female leatherbacks make several different sounds. Some of the sounds are like sighs, and some are like belches. Using an underwater television system, researchers have been able to view leatherback turtles under attack. When attacked, the turtles seemed to roar. Scientists do not know if these sounds are signals sent out to other leatherback turtles.

Some researchers have reported that it is likely that female leatherbacks, like other animals, give off a certain scent to communicate that they are ready to mate. Studies of leatherbacks indicate that the female has just one mate for each **clutch** of eggs. This is not true of other kinds of turtles. The eggs of most turtles have multiple fathers. Yet unlike birds and other kinds of animals, the turtles do not seem to bond as couples any more than they do as groups. The couple does not seem to help each other much. Unlike other species, the female leatherback is not given gifts from the male. She is not helped with the care of the eggs. There is little need to communicate.

The need for communication among leatherbacks seems to be limited when it comes to hunting as well. To survive, leatherbacks must hunt almost constantly. A leatherback's daily schedule is a response to the movements of jellyfish. The jellyfish are the turtles' favorite prey. Several studies have shown that the turtles spend most of their time diving. Researchers attached devices to female turtles while they were nesting. When the females returned to the sea, the devices helped scientists learn how deep and how long the turtles were diving. In one study, ten females were almost always diving. They stayed underwater for about ten minutes each time and made about five dives every hour. The turtles would come up to breathe and then immediately go back down again. They did this most of the day and night. During the middle of the day, they spent more time at the surface of the water. In the evening, the leatherbacks did not dive as deep. In the early morning, they dove to greater and greater depths. This activity cycle has been linked to the leatherback's desire to find its favorite food rather than group behavior that is coordinated through communication. The jellyfish tend to rise toward the ocean's surface at night and drop down again in early morning. At midday, when the jellyfish are farthest from the surface, the turtles seem to rest near the surface, where the Sun warms the water.

When hatched, the young run toward the shine of sunlight or moonlight on the water. The light seems to be their signal to move.

Turtle Truths

Despite the current lack of knowledge about leatherback communication, it is clear that they migrate thousands of miles (kilometers) each year in certain patterns. They have some kind of tracking system.

Female leatherbacks do not stay on land to help their offspring. When the hatchlings appear, their mother is not around.

Body Studies

It is not known for certain how the leatherback tracks other turtles or communicates its needs. The leatherback turtle is a deep-sea mystery in most ways, but studying its body could help lead to answers. Its survival, in the future as it was in the past, is likely to be linked to the turtle's size and special way of warming itself. Watching for changes in its covering and coloring could help researchers understand any changes in the oceans.

Size

Most adult leatherbacks weigh between 440 and 2,000 pounds (200 and 900 kg), and their upper shell is about 5 feet (1.5 m) long. Male and female leatherbacks are about the same size, but males have a longer tail. Researchers are not yet sure why some of the turtles thrive more than others. Knowing why might lead to clues for their survival.

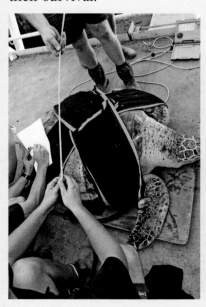

Temperature

Leatherbacks are reptiles, but they are not true **ectotherms**. An ectotherm's body temperature depends on the temperature of its environment. Leatherbacks often are found in colder waters than other sea turtles. Scientists found that leatherbacks are usually warmer than the water in which they swim. Some scientists have come to believe that dinosaurs also had this characteristic.

Covering

The part of a turtle's shell that covers its back is called the **carapace**. The section that covers its belly is called the **plastron**. The carapace of the leatherback is about 1.6 inches (4 cm) thick. It is made of tough, oily tissue. It feels like rubber and has ridges. The ridges run lengthwise from the turtle's front legs toward its tail. There are seven ridges on the turtle's back and five ridges on its underside. The carapace and plastron sections of the shell do not join at a sharp angle as in most turtles. This gives the leatherback turtle a barrel-shaped appearance.

Coloring

Adult leatherbacks do not all have the same color pattern, but their leathery skin is mostly black with pale spots. Their belly spots turn pinkish when they are out of the water. This shows that blood is flowing to cool the skin. Leatherback turtle hatchlings appear black when seen from a distance, but on closer inspection, white markings can be seen along the edges of the flippers. The back of a hatchling has white stripes. The stripes are actually rows of white scales. These scales disappear as the hatchlings grow up. The white spots become less distinct as the turtle ages.

Take a Stand

· Debate ·   · Research ·

Should people be restricted from using the turtles' nesting beaches?

The underside of the leatherback's body can be injured by sharp rocks or plants, so the turtle is attracted to soft sandy beaches that tend to **erode**. In some places, leatherbacks' favorite beaches are also favorites for people.

FOR

1. Governments can easily set up rules to help people and turtles share a beach area, such as not allowing vehicles on the sand.
2. Most people have no trouble sharing prime beaches with the turtles once the people are educated about the need to leave space for the turtles to place their eggs.

AGAINST

1. There is not unlimited beach property, and the needs of humans come first. Development of beachfront areas leads to jobs, which benefits human families.
2. The main dangers to leatherbacks are pollution and injuries from fishing lures. Rather than concentrating on beaches, people who want to help the turtles should be looking at those problems.

Turtle Truths

It takes as long as a decade for hatchlings to return to beaches as adults. This is one reason why it has taken a while for people to realize that the population of leatherbacks is endangered.

The hatchlings emerge about 60 to 65 days after the eggs have been placed in the body pit.

Mating and Birth

The nesting season for leatherbacks varies by location. In general, leatherback turtles in the Atlantic and the Caribbean nest from March to July. Leatherbacks in the Pacific nest from October to January. The **gestation period** for sea turtles is about two months. At the end of this period, the mother climbs up on a beach to make a nest and lay her eggs. If the eggs are undisturbed, dozens of baby turtles hatch from these eggs about two months later. Females usually nest at night. They are out of the water for only 60 to 90 minutes.

On the shore, the leatherback female makes a hole in the sand, which is called a body pit. At the back of the body pit, the female digs the nest hole with her rear flippers. Some sea turtles make shallow body pits, but leatherbacks make medium to deep pits. The nest is usually made just above the high-tide mark so that newly hatched turtles will not have far to go in order to reach the water. Once the nest is dug, she lays between 45 and 160 eggs in it. Then, using her flippers, she fills the rest of the nest with sand. She pats the sand down firmly with her flippers and then sweeps more sand over the area. This action makes the nest more difficult for predators to find.

The female then goes back to the water. About ten days later, she returns to the beach and lays more eggs in a new nest. She usually makes four to five nests per season, but she may make up to 11 nests in the four-month nesting period. This process is exhausting. The number of nests helps to explain why leatherbacks nest every two to three years, rather than annually.

From an Expert

"Sea turtles are beautiful complex creatures, mysterious enough to become addicting for the biologist, absorbing for anyone to watch, and of great value for their eggs, meat, shell, and leather."
- Dr. Nicholas Mrosovsky

Dr. Nicolas Mrosovsky is a professor in the departments of zoology, physiology, and psychology at the University of Toronto. He has been studying sea turtles for decades and has written much about them, including the book *Conserving Sea Turtles*.

Baby Leatherbacks

The outside of a leatherback's eggs are leathery. They are not as easily broken as the eggs of a chicken. This feature allows the female to leave the eggs buried in the sand, rather than guard them. After the female lays her eggs, the young leatherbacks are left on their own. In all likelihood, a leatherback hatchling never sees its mother or father, even when grown. When the baby leatherbacks hatch, they rest for a few days. Then, they scramble up through the sand toward the surface. As the hatchlings move upward together, a keen observer on the sand can see a small depression of sand above the nest. This is how to tell that the young have hatched and will likely be coming out of the sand that night.

The combined movement of all the hatchlings moving together at the same time makes the sand flow. In this way, the hatchlings help one another. The flowing sand is easier for the hatchlings to move through. They move together until the Sun's heat in the top layer of sand stops them from climbing to the surface. They then wait for better conditions. When the sand cools, they emerge. This is why it is usually nighttime when the hatchlings reach the surface. The hatchlings then scramble toward the sea. Once the young leatherbacks reach the water, they swim several miles (kilometers) offshore. That is to say, the young that are not eaten by sharks and other large fish swim out that far. It is estimated that only one in a thousand hatchlings reaches adulthood. If a hatchling makes it past the dangers in shallow water, a current picks it up and carries it out to sea.

Each young sea turtle is on its own from the very beginning. A hatchling is about 3.5 inches (8.9 centimeters) long. Its shell length is usually about 2 to 2.7 inches (5.1 to 6.9 cm). It weighs about 1.3 to 1.7 ounces (36.8 to 48.2 grams) at birth. When the baby leatherbacks hatch, they have distinct white blotches on their skin. They have distinct white ridges on their shells. They are born with huge flippers that are as long as the shell. The flippers of hatchling leatherbacks are bigger than those of any other sea turtle hatchlings. The hatchlings have scales on their bodies, but these disappear as they become adults.

The exact time it takes for the eggs to hatch varies depending on factors such as the temperature of the sand.

Turtle Truths

Leatherbacks nest in the tropics during hurricane season. Hurricanes can sometimes create waves and wind that destroy almost all the nests on a beach.

When the hatchlings first emerge from their eggs, they eat the yolk of their eggs for energy.

Development

The leatherback turtle and the flatback turtle of Australia have the largest eggs and hatchlings of any sea turtles. The leatherback turtle's eggs are about 2 inches (5 cm) in diameter, and they weigh between 1.5 and 2.3 pounds (70 and 103 g). Leatherback turtle eggs are covered by a special white shell that is somewhat flexible. The eggs that will produce hatchlings resemble billiard balls. Each nest typically has about 80 eggs that are able to grow into hatchlings. These eggs rest with 30 or so smaller eggs that will never hatch. Once the eggs are laid, they **incubate** in the sand for 50 to 78 days before they hatch. Warmer weather usually means a shorter incubation period.

In nests where the temperature is between 84.2° Fahrenheit and 55.9°F (29° Celsius and 13.3°C), about half the hatchlings are male and half are female. When the temperatures are cooler, more males are hatched. When it is warmer, more females are hatched. Although the hatchlings are hardy, they face many dangers on the beach and in the ocean. Birds and other predators hunt the hatchlings as soon as they reach the surface of the beach.

Hatchlings that reach the sea never leave the water during the early stages of their lives. For this reason, very little is known about **juvenile** leatherbacks. Scientists call this period "the lost year." No one knows for sure what the juveniles eat, but scientists think that juvenile leatherback turtles, like adults, eat mainly jellyfish. It seems that the juveniles stay in tropical waters in the early stages. Some studies indicate that they may stay in warmer waters through the first five years of life. The young leatherbacks do not move on to cooler water until they reach a length of 3 feet (1 m) or so.

It is difficult for scientists to learn much more about the early stages of a leatherback's life. Researchers attach devices to adult turtles in order to track and study them. This practice is known as tagging. Most of the tagging devices that scientists use, however, are too big to put on young turtles.

A leatherback is considered to be an adult when its shell is about 4 feet (1.2 m) long. This is the earliest age at which it can reproduce. Some researchers believe this size is reached within three years. Others say that **maturation** more likely occurs within six years. Yet others find that the turtles are not fully mature for 12 to 14 years.

The first hatchlings to come out of their shells produce movements that encourage the other hatchlings to break out as well.

Hatchlings break through their eggshells on their own, using a special tooth called a caruncle. This tooth falls out shortly afterward.

The strong front flippers help the turtle slide across the sand.

Habitat

Unlike other sea turtles that often feed near the shore, leatherbacks spend most of their lives far from the shore in the open ocean. Every few years a female leatherback will return to a beach in a warmer climate in order to nest. The majority of a turtle's time, however, is spent in cooler waters far away from the coast.

The ocean is the leatherback's main habitat, and the range a turtle covers in the water is enormous. Not only does the leatherback travel vast distances across the water, but it moves through many different depths of the ocean. A leatherback is at home while floating on the surface of the water and while diving deep toward the ocean floor.

Organizing the Ocean

Earth is home to millions of different **organisms**, all of which have specific survival needs. These organisms rely on their environment, or the place where they live, for their survival. All plants and animals have relationships with their environment. They interact with the environment itself, as well as the other plants and animals within the environment. These interactions create **ecosystems**.

Ecosystems can be broken down into levels of organization. These levels range from a single plant or animal to many species of plants and animals living together in an area.

Organism
A single organism

Population
Many organisms of the same species

Community
Several species living together

Biosphere
Planet Earth and all of its living things

Ecosystem
Many species of plants and animals in an area

Fish called remoras have been known to hitchhike on strong leatherback turtles.

Range

The leatherback turtle is found in a wide range around the world. Unlike some turtles that spend their lives near where they were born, leatherback turtles travel great distances. Some have been reported to have traveled more than 7,400 miles (12,000 km) from the beach where they usually nest. They make their nests in the tropics, but when they are not nesting, they can travel as far north as Canada and the Barents Sea, which borders Norway and Russia. Scientists believe leatherbacks find their way by sensing changes in Earth's magnetic field.

In order to find out how far leatherbacks traveled, scientists once had to be lucky enough to find a turtle that they had already tagged. When one of these turtles was found in a certain place, no one knew how it got there. Did it swim in a straight line from the point where it was first tagged, or did it travel to many different places before being located the second time?

Now scientists can use satellites to help them track how turtles travel. They first attach a transmitter to the leatherback turtle when she comes out of the water to nest. When she returns to the water, the satellite picks up the signal from the turtle's transmitter. In one study, scientists followed eight turtles using satellites. All the turtles had laid their eggs on the same nesting beach in Costa Rica. Even though they were not traveling together, they followed a similar travel route. The transmitters stopped giving signals within three months, but in that time, one of the turtles had traveled 1,727 miles (2,780 km) in 87 days. She had an average speed of about 20 miles (32 km) per day.

Recently, leatherbacks were tracked in the South Atlantic for the first time. The routes they took led directly through fishing areas.

Female leatherbacks most often return to the same beach but will move to a beach nearby if the conditions are right. The turtles look for soft sand and a high slope.

Migration

In the early days of turtle tracking, one adult leatherback turtle was tagged in French Guiana, South America, and seen again off the coast of Newfoundland, Canada. The fast-moving turtle had traveled at least 3,107 miles (5,002 km) in 128 days. Another leatherback reached Mozambique, 624 miles (1,004 km) away from where it was tagged a year before in Tongaland, South Africa.

Most early reports about the turtles' migration patterns came from the discovery of a turtle that was previously tagged. The leatherback that was originally tagged in French Guiana was part of a group of several tagged turtles that were found elsewhere. Their recapture sites included Ghana, in West Africa. They also included a recapture site on the New Jersey shore. The female leatherback turtle caught in Ghana had traveled at least 3,700 miles (5,957 km) in less than one year.

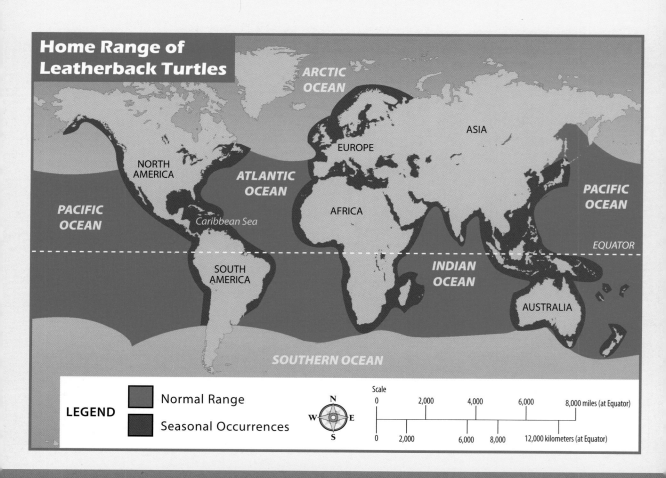

Home Range of Leatherback Turtles

LEGEND
Normal Range
Seasonal Occurrences

Scale

One turtle that was tagged while nesting in the Virgin Islands was found 85 days later in New Jersey. She had traveled at least 1,934 miles (3,113 km), averaging more than 22.7 miles (36.6 km) per day. These distances astounded researchers, but the records keep getting broken. More recently, one female was tagged in Indonesia and followed to the U.S. state of Oregon. She traveled all the way across the Pacific Ocean and started back again. She was followed for 647 days and 12,774 miles (20,558 km) before the tracking signal was lost.

To better understand the routes that the turtles follow, researchers recently placed tags on female leatherbacks that nest on the Pacific coast of Costa Rica, in Central America. Then, they followed the females' movements, using satellite trackers. The turtles followed a relatively narrow route through the water. They traveled past the Galápagos Islands. After they crossed the **equator** into the Southern Hemisphere, they stayed for a while in the waters of the South Pacific. The movement occurred from February to April. Turtles were also studied in the South Atlantic. Twenty-five females were tagged at a breeding site in Gabon. Two of the groups moved from Gabon to the southwest and southeast Atlantic. Another group traveled straight across the Atlantic from Africa to South America. The newer studies show that the turtles have a wider variety of travel routes than first thought. The research points to the need for international cooperation in the study of these ocean animals.

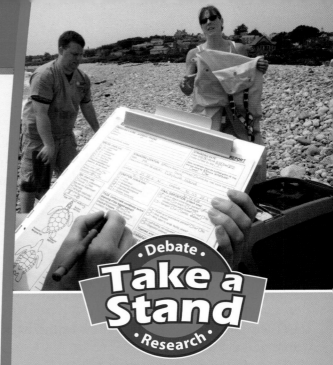

Take a Stand

·Debate· ·Research·

Should the tagging of turtles be stopped because the information tagging provides is not very useful?

Scientists tag leatherback turtles and note where they show up to try to understand how the turtles travel. Some people say tagging wastes money and time because the data has limited value.

FOR

1. When tagged turtles are not found, they are often assumed to be dead. Perhaps the tagged turtles simply did not return to the same nesting beach. Or the tags may have fallen off. Too much is assumed.
2. Tagging turtles for no specific reason creates useless data. Research studies have the greatest value when they are designed to prove very specific points.

AGAINST

1. A good computer program can account for any number of mistaken ideas about the tags and the turtles. A program can include a margin of error.
2. Data analysis is a rapidly changing field. We should collect as much information as possible, even if the importance of some of it cannot be understood immediately.

Diet

Adult leatherback turtles are **carnivores**, but the jaws of leatherback turtles are not very strong. Because of their lack of jaw strength, leatherback turtles feed on animals with soft bodies. They feed mainly on different types of jellyfish.

Sea turtles have no teeth, but the upper jaw of the leatherback is shaped like the letter *W*, and the lower jaw has one center point that fits in the middle notch on the upper jaw. Leatherbacks also have sharp edges on their jaws. These features allow leatherbacks to hold and cut their prey.

The Portuguese man-o-war has stingers filled with toxins, but they cannot cut into the leatherback's thick skin.

Part of the mouth and the throat of a leatherback is lined with backward-facing **papillae**, which are like soft spines. The papillae are usually more than 1 inch (2.5 cm) long. The papillae help keep slippery jellyfish from sliding back up after they have been swallowed. Most animals digest much of their food in their stomach, but leatherbacks have a small stomach. Instead, they get most of the **nutrients** from the food they eat while the food is in their small intestine. Leatherbacks shed tears as a way to rid themselves of extra salt they take in.

There are more than 200 species of jellyfish living in Earth's oceans. These marine species are mainly composed of water, but somehow these creatures provide enough nutrients for the turtles to get the food energy needed to swim long distances and dive almost constantly. Some scientists say that the turtles must eat 50 or so large jellyfish each day in order to stay active and healthy.

Sometimes leatherbacks eat other animals, such as sea squirts. They have been known to eat squid and fish, among other sea creatures. They are reported to also sometimes eat algae and sea grass, but these are likely to be eaten accidentally when the turtle eats other things. Leatherback turtles can even eat the Portuguese man-o-war, a jellyfish that has organs that give a poisonous sting.

The turtles have also been known to mistake trash, such as plastic bags, for floating jellyfish. Some leatherback turtles have been found with more than 10 pounds of plastic inside. A recent study found that more than one-third of leatherbacks that were stranded on beaches had plastic in their systems. The plastic blocks the turtle's gut. The animal becomes bloated and eventually dies.

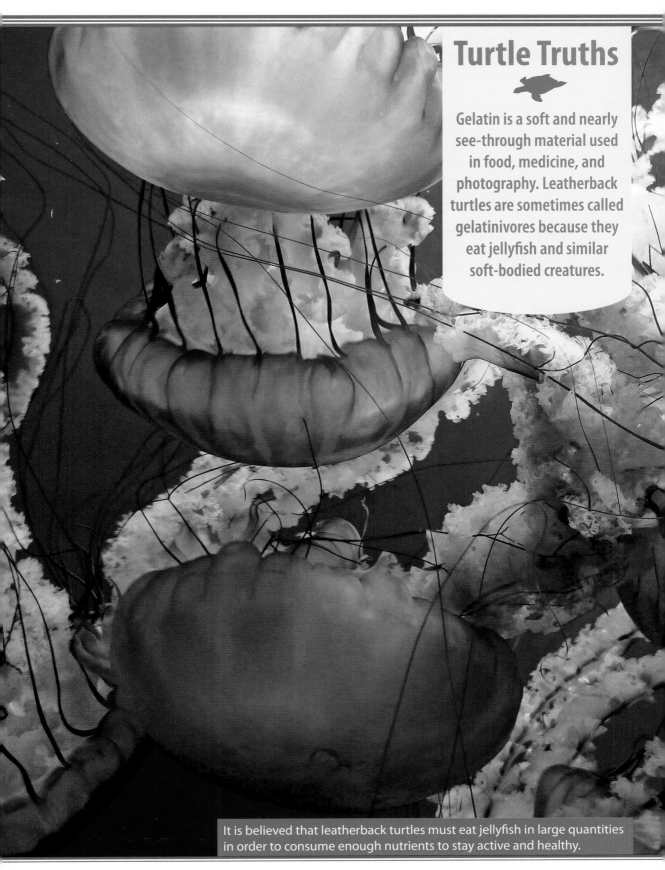

Turtle Truths

Gelatin is a soft and nearly see-through material used in food, medicine, and photography. Leatherback turtles are sometimes called gelatinivores because they eat jellyfish and similar soft-bodied creatures.

It is believed that leatherback turtles must eat jellyfish in large quantities in order to consume enough nutrients to stay active and healthy.

The Food Cycle

A food cycle shows how energy in the form of food is passed from one living thing to another. Leatherback turtles are a part of the food cycle from the time they are inside their eggs through to adulthood. During all the stages of their development, leatherback turtles affect the lives of many other animals. In the diagram below, the arrows show the flow of energy from one living thing to the next through a **food web**.

Tertiary Consumers
While still in their eggs, leatherbacks are a food source for animals such as monitor lizards and wild boars. As hatchlings, they are eaten by vultures and jaguars. Adults are sometimes eaten by killer whales.

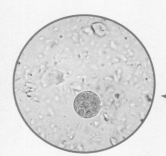

Parasites
Leatherback turtles are hosts for parasites such as amoeba. The turtles carry creatures such as barnacles on their shells.

Secondary Consumers
Jellyfish are the main food source for leatherbacks. Leatherbacks, in turn, provide food for other living things.

Producers
Tiny plants and animals called plankton live in the ocean. They get their nutrients from the water and the ocean floor.

Primary Consumers
Plankton are the main part of the diet eaten by jellyfish. The jellyfish are then eaten by leatherback turtles.

Decomposers
When a turtle dies, its body is broken down by decomposers. This adds nutrients to the ocean and helps plankton thrive.

Take a Stand
· Debate ·
· Research ·

Should people be allowed to eat some leatherback turtle eggs?
Many people think that harvesting eggs helps people without hurting the turtles because there are so many eggs in each nest.

FOR

1. In nature, many turtle eggs are wasted. Some nests are laid below the high-tide mark, and the eggs are doomed anyway. If the eggs are not going to hatch, it makes sense to use them.
2. When local people are allowed to take eggs, they will value the turtles more. They may report **poaching**, as well as any new nesting activity.

AGAINST

1. When animals are endangered, we should save as many as possible. Scientists do not know how many eggs can be harvested without harming the leatherback population.
2. It is impossible to tell apart eggs that were legally collected and those that were poached. Allowing legal harvests helps poachers get away with their crime.

Turtle Truths

The eggs of the leatherback turtle are most at risk. Not only do many animals enjoy eating the eggs, but human activity can destroy the nests.

Humans in many parts of the world consider turtle eggs a delicacy and sell the eggs at markets.

Competition

Leatherbacks are solitary creatures, and little is known about their interactions, so not much has been established regarding competition among them. Leatherback turtles will swim for thousands of miles (kilometers) to find water that is filled with jellyfish and other food. The oceans are wide, open spaces, and there is plenty of food for the turtles out at sea, so competition among them is minimal.

There may be some competition to win mates, but this, too, appears to be minimal. Males have been seen on video fighting for females, but the males fight the females rather than each other. On beaches, females sometimes destroy the nests of turtles that have nested earlier, when they dig their own nests. This appears to be accidental, however, and the other females are not aware that anything has happened, as they have laid the eggs and returned to the water.

Leatherbacks sometimes compete with smaller turtles for the same food sources, but the leatherbacks have the advantage. The main challenges to leatherbacks come from other species. Juvenile leatherbacks face danger on land and in the water from predators such as jaguars and sharks. The eggs are sometimes eaten by dogs, jackals, wild boars, and pigs. In South Africa, Australia, and Sri Lanka, monitor lizards also feed on the eggs. Once hatchlings have reached the surface of the nest, and while they run to the sea, they have to deal with other enemies. During this short time, they can be attacked by birds, including vultures. They may also be eaten by land animals such as skunks. Once the hatchlings reach the water, they may be eaten by sea birds or by fish or squid.

Humans are the biggest challenge to leatherbacks and other endangered sea turtles. People in some parts of the world use turtle oil to light lamps and to oil wooden boats. Human activity poses a challenge at every stage of the leatherback's life. The turtles are in danger of fishing equipment when they leave the shore as hatchlings and when they are young and growing within the warmer tropical waters. In all these cases, the turtles do not struggle with competition from other turtles and sea animals. They are instead facing danger from the environment and the humans who affect it.

Crabs hunt for juvenile sea turtles and pounce on them as the baby turtles make their way to the sea.

Turtle Truths

The meat of leatherback turtles can be poisonous to humans and other animals. If people were able to regularly eat leatherbacks, the danger to the turtles would probably be greater.

When beaches are filled with tire tracks or other alterations, the turtles can find it hard to return to the water after nesting.

Leatherback Turtles with Other Animals

In the water, adult sea turtles are sometimes attacked by sharks, though they are not usually killed by them. Adult leatherbacks will try to ram into the shark, bite at it, swim rapidly around, swim upside down on the surface of the water, and splash on the surface. Adult leatherbacks are, however, sometimes attacked and eaten by killer whales. On land, nesting turtles are sometimes killed by animals such as jaguars.

Throughout a leatherback's life cycle, in the water or on land, humans are a danger. In a few areas, the drop in leatherback numbers seems to be a direct result of uncontrolled egg collections by people looking for food. Adult leatherbacks are not poached as often as many other sea turtle species, but their illegal capture is still a problem. Many additional leatherback deaths are considered accidental. Adult leatherbacks drown while caught in fishing nets, unable to reach the surface to breathe. Adults and juveniles are also killed when caught by shrimp trawlers. They are sometimes caught on fishing lines meant for tuna, swordfish, sailfish, and sharks. They can also be killed in collisions with boats.

Humans can pollute the ocean and ruin nesting sites. Plastic garbage that lands in the ocean can be deadly for a sea turtle that mistakes the items for food. The plastic may block the throat or get stuck in the intestines. If a female sea turtle is disturbed when she is crawling up the beach to make her nest, she may return to the ocean without laying eggs. She may also pick a bad nesting site or not make a proper nest.

From an Expert

Dr. Karen Eckert is a biologist who has spent many years studying sea turtles and helping to conserve them. She is Executive Director of the Wider Caribbean Sea Turtle Conservation Network (WIDECAST).

"In virtually every corner of the globe, wild sea turtle populations are declining as a result of habitat loss or degradation, overexploitation, incidental catch, and pollution." - Dr. Karen Eckert

Folklore

A man named Aesop was said to be the author of famous Greek fables from long ago. One of his stories is about a race between a tortoise and a hare. The turtle is the winner. The quick-footed hare learns that "slow and steady" wins the race. In most fables and folklore, turtles are seen in a positive way. They are sometimes seen to be protectors of people and are often linked to stories about the creation of the world. Many American Indians explain the beginning of the world with stories involving a turtle. Some even call North America "turtle island."

The turtle appears in the tales and beliefs of many different cultures. One folktale from New Guinea explains how that island was created by a sea turtle. The turtle wanted somewhere to rest when she grew tired of swimming. She brought rocks and sand to build a hill in the ocean. When she was getting the rocks, she found a man living alone in a cave beneath the sea. He wanted a wife and family. The turtle took him to her island. Then she swam across the sea to another island and found a woman who wanted a husband. The turtle brought her to the island to live with the man. The couple raised a family, and they eventually populated the whole island.

There is a Hawai'ian legend about a young turtle named Kauila whose parents were two magical turtles. Kauila could become a human girl and then change back into a turtle. She would change into a girl to play with children and then return to an underwater spring to sleep. When she returned to her spring, she would become a turtle again. Kauila protected the village children from drowning, and her spring gave them fresh water.

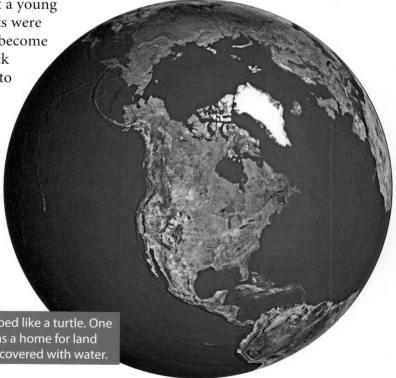

Some people say North America is shaped like a turtle. One legend says that a turtle gave its back as a home for land animals during a time when Earth was covered with water.

Myth	**VS**	Fact
 Sea turtles live only in the tropics.		Some sea turtle species, such as the hawksbill, green, and flatback turtle, do live in the tropics. Other species of sea turtles spend at least part of their lives in other areas. Although the leatherback nests in the tropics, it spends much of its life in nontropical regions.
 Turtles are slow.		Sea turtles are slow on land, but in the water they can move quite quickly. Sea turtles are known to swim at speeds of up to 3 miles (4.8 km) per hour. Male sea turtles almost never leave the sea after entering it as hatchlings. The observation that turtles are slow comes from seeing the females on sand. While nesting, the females move slowly on land. This places them in danger from predators.
 Turtles weep when they leave their eggs in the sand.		Although tears fall from a female sea turtle's eyes as she lays her eggs, she is not sad. The tears are a way for her body to get rid of salt. The tears fall from her eyes in the water too, but they cannot be seen by the human eye or by cameras.

In China, the turtle is considered one of four creatures guarding the four points of the compass.

Status

Leatherbacks are considered an endangered species. At current rates of decline, these sea turtles may die out. The largest remaining sites for nesting are along the coast of western Africa and the northern section of South America. Minor sites can be found in the Caribbean, mainly around the U.S. Virgin Islands and Puerto Rico. Some sites are found around Florida as well.

Pacific leatherback populations have decreased 80 percent in the past decade. Around the world, there have been numerous signs of decline among leatherback turtle populations. In Terengganu, Malaysia, there was a 98 percent drop in the number of nesting turtles over a 30-year period. This was almost all due to a poorly controlled egg harvest. The situation was doubly tragic because the government believed it was managing the harvest properly by buying back some of the harvested eggs from harvesters. These eggs were to be hatched artificially to keep the population of turtles strong. The officials in charge did not buy enough eggs, so the population dropped.

The Atlantic nesting populations have been troubled as well. In 1979, the Virgin Islands were declared a critical habitat for the species. More recently, the population of leatherbacks in Costa Rica fell dramatically. In 1988 and 1989, researchers counted 1,367 nesting turtles. In 1998 and 1999, scientists counted only 117. At another beach, in Mexico, numbers dropped from 75,000 in the early 1980s to 1,000 by the beginning of the 21st century.

On a more positive note, in 2007, the National Oceanic and Atmospheric Administration (NOAA) asked to have the West Coast of the United States declared a critical habitat. In early 2012, large areas of the coast were officially placed under protection. New protections are also being considered for the coasts of Puerto Rico. Meanwhile, researchers have seen a small increase in the number of leatherbacks nesting on Atlantic beaches. In the Caribbean, the leatherback population appears to be increasing. The turtles that are found there, however, are in numbers much lower than the Pacific groups at their height. Scientists are investigating the growing populations to find clues to help the species in places where the number of turtles is continuing to drop.

Turtle Truths

All of the sea turtle species are endangered. Six of these species reside off the coast of the United States. A large oil spill in the Gulf of Mexico in 2010 killed many turtles in the Gulf.

Scientists are active on beaches during the nesting seasons to find out more about the leatherback turtle.

Turtle Truths

Beach patrols are trained to relocate the eggs laid in nests below the high-tide mark.

In many areas, members of the community are trained to look for poachers and to collect data on the turtles found on the beaches.

Saving the Leatherback

Some sea turtles are used to make turtleshell jewelry and other expensive items. For example, poachers look for the olive ridley turtle because they can make leather from its skin. Fortunately, leatherbacks do not have valuable skin, and people avoid leatherback meat because it contains poisons. Laws against poaching, however, are helping all sea turtles, including the leatherback.

Fishing laws are also helping the turtles. In U.S. waters, shrimp trawlers must be equipped with special devices. These devices allow turtles to escape from the trawl instead of drowning in it. In a fishing method called longlining, long lines hold thousands of hooks out over many miles (kilometers) of water. The lures attract and kill many sea turtles by accident. This method is mainly used by Chinese, Japanese, and Korean fishers to catch valued fish such as swordfish. Numerous groups are working to raise awareness of the issue and to reach turtle-friendly agreements on fishing in international waters.

When people erect buildings on beaches, they change the shoreline to protect their property from erosion. They use sandbags, cement, and other methods to protect their development. This often makes it impossible for the turtles to climb up on the beach. In other areas, people try to rebuild parts of beaches that have been lost to erosion. The sand on the rebuilt beaches can be too loosely packed or too hard. This often results in nests being buried too deep or the beach being too hard for the turtles to use to dig nests. New construction can be made in ways that protect both the property and the leatherback.

From an Expert

"If a carefully planned, [broad] strategy were worked out, sea turtles could no doubt be permanently saved. . . . Without such a strategy, however, we are likely to lose some of the species completely before much more time goes by."
- Dr. Archie Carr

Dr. Archie Carr was a professor in the department of zoology at the University of Florida. He directed the green turtle research program in Tortuguero, Costa Rica.

Back from the Brink

Hatchlings are easy prey, and they can die from exposure. Once hatchling sea turtles emerge from their nests, they must get to the ocean as quickly as possible to avoid predators. They move toward the light that is reflected off the water. On a beach that is surrounded by buildings or used by humans, the light a hatchling heads for may be someone's front porch light, a campfire, or a highway. Or there may be tire tracks and garbage on the sand that make the hatchling's movement difficult or impossible.

It is important to respect the turtles' habitat. Never drive on a beach during nesting season, and do not walk on a sea turtle beach at night. Vehicles driven over nests may pack the sand down so hard that hatchlings have difficulty reaching the surface. Nesting turtles may be scared by human activity and turn back to the water without laying eggs. Make sure all lights near turtle beaches are turned off at night. In addition, make certain nothing is left the beach that might interfere with a turtle's movements. Even lawn chairs and umbrellas can get in the way of nesting turtles or hatchlings. Stay away from nesting turtles, and do not pick up or disturb hatchlings. Do not go near marked sea turtle nests. If you see anyone bothering a turtle or a turtle nest, report it immediately. Even people who live far from the turtles' beaches can help. Do not throw garbage into the ocean. Garbage, especially plastics, may look enough like jellyfish that turtles may eat it and get sick or die.

For more information on efforts to save the leatherback turtle, contact:

The Leatherback Trust
161 Merlon Avenue
Haddonfield, New Jersey 08033

The turtles require clean water and beaches. Understanding turtle behavior, and changing human behavior, can change the future for turtles.

Activity

Debating helps people think about ideas thoughtfully and carefully. When people debate, two sides take a different viewpoint on a subject. Each side takes turns presenting arguments to support its view.

Use the Take a Stand sections found throughout this book as a starting point for debate topics. Organize your friends or classmates into two teams. One team will argue in favor of the topic, and the other will argue against. Each team should research the issue thoroughly using reliable sources of information, including books, scientific journals, and trustworthy websites. Take notes of important facts that support your side of the debate. Prepare your argument using these facts to support your opinion.

During the debate, the members of each team are given a set amount of time to make their arguments. The team arguing the For side goes first. They have five minutes to present their case. All members of the team should participate equally. Then, the team arguing the Against side presents its arguments. Each team should take notes of the main points the other team argues.

After both teams have made their arguments, they get three minutes to prepare their **rebuttals**. Teams review their notes from the previous round. The teams focus on trying to disprove each of the main points made by the other team using solid facts. Each team gets three minutes to make its rebuttal. The team arguing the Against side goes first. Students and teachers watching the debate serve as judges. They should try to judge the debate fairly using a standard score sheet, such as the example below.

Criteria	Rate: 1-10	Sample Comments
1. Were the arguments well organized?	8	logical arguments, easy to follow
2. Did team members participate equally?	9	divided time evenly between members
3. Did team members speak loudly and clearly?	3	some members were difficult to hear
4. Were rebuttals specific to the other team's arguments?	6	rebuttals were specific, more facts needed
5. Was respect shown for the other team?	10	all members showed respect to the other team

Quiz

2. What are the hard sections on the leatherback turtle's shell called?

3. What name is given to a large group of floating turtles?

1. How did the leatherback get its name?

4. How often do leatherback females return to their nesting sites?

5. Why do leatherback turtles rest at midday?

6. How long is the gestation period of leatherbacks?

7. When turtle eggs are kept between 84.2°F and 55.9°F (29°C and 13°C), what proportion of hatchlings are males?

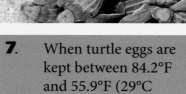

9. What do animals that are gelatinivores eat?

8. Why do leatherback turtles cry?

10. In which ocean have leatherbacks declined the most?

Answers:

1. It has leathery skin all over. 2. scutes 3. a flotilla 4. every two to three years 5. The jellyfish are farthest from the surface then. 6. about two months 7. half 8. to get rid of excess salt 9. soft-bodied creatures 10. the Pacific

Key Words

carapace: the part of the shell of the turtle that covers its back

carnivores: animals that eat other animals

clutch: all the eggs in one nest

ecosystems: communities of living things and resources

ectotherms: animals whose body temperature depends on the temperature of their surrounding environment

endangered: in danger of becoming extinct, or no longer surviving in the world

equator: an imaginary line around the center of Earth, dividing the northern and southern hemispheres

erode: to be worn away by rain, wind, and other natural forces

family: one of eight major ranks used to classify animals, between order and genus

flotilla: a Spanish word for a large group of migrant turtles drifting or swimming together in the open ocean

food web: connecting food chains that show how energy flows from one organism to another through diet

gestation period: the length of time a female is pregnant with young

hatchling: a young sea turtle that has just come out of its shell

incubate: to keep eggs warm for hatching

juvenile: young or immature

maturation: the process of changing from a juvenile into an adult

nutrients: substances in food that animals need to live, grow, and be active

organisms: forms of life

papillae: small projecting body parts, like soft spines

plastron: the part of the turtle's shell that covers the belly region

poaching: a type of hunting that is not legal, in which animals are killed or their eggs are stolen, often to be sold for profit

rebuttals: attempts to counter, or disprove, an argument

scutes: external plates forming a bony covering

species: groups of individuals with common characteristics

Index

Log on to www.av2books.com

AV² by Weigl brings you media enhanced books that support active learning. Go to www.av2books.com, and enter the special code found on page 2 of this book. You will gain access to enriched and enhanced content that supplements and complements this book. Content includes video, audio, weblinks, quizzes, a slide show, and activities.

Audio
Listen to sections of the book read aloud.

Video
Watch informative video clips.

Embedded Weblinks
Gain additional information for research.

Try This!
Complete activities and hands-on experiments.

WHAT'S ONLINE?

Try This!	**Embedded Weblinks**	**Video**	**EXTRA FEATURES**
Chart the levels of organization within the biosphere.	Learn more about leatherback turtles.	Watch a video about leatherback turtles.	**Audio** Listen to sections of the book read aloud.
Map leatherback turtle habitats around the world.	Read about leatherback turtle conservation efforts.	See a leatherback turtle nesting on a sandy beach.	
Complete a food web for leatherback turtles.	Find out more about leatherback turtle habitats.		**Key Words** Study vocabulary, and complete a matching word activity.
Label and describe the parts of the leatherback turtle.	Discover more fascinating facts about leatherback turtles.		**Slide Show** View images and captio and prepare a presentat
Classify leatherback turtles using a classification diagram.	Learn more about what you can do to help save leatherback turtles.		**Quizzes** Test your knowledge.

AV² was built to bridge the gap between print and digital. We encourage you to tell us what you like and what you want to see in the future.

Sign up to be an AV² Ambassador at www.av2books.com/ambassador.

Due to the dynamic nature of the Internet, some of the URLs and activities provided as part of AV² by Weigl may have changed or ceased to exist. AV² by Weigl accepts no responsibility for any such changes. All media enhanced books are regularly monitored to update addresses and sites in a timely manner. Contact AV² by Weigl at 1-866-649-3445 or av2books@weigl.com with any questions, comments, or feedback.